Mary Broad By Linda Crystal

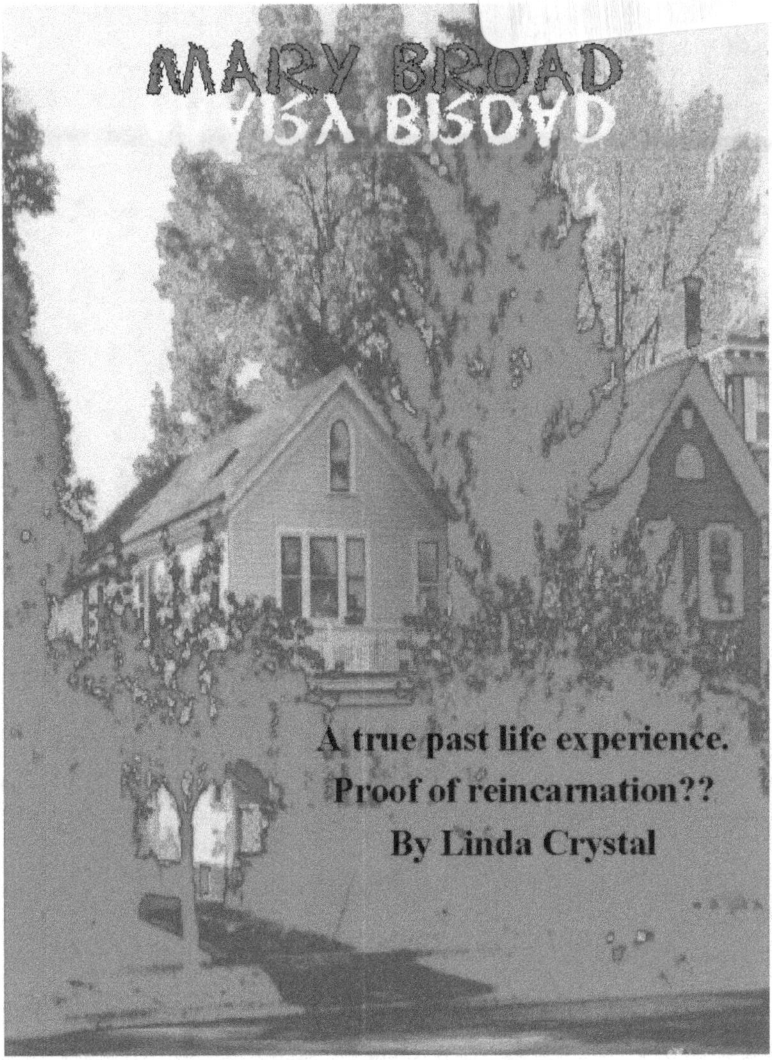
MARY BROAD
A true past life experience.
Proof of reincarnation??
By Linda Crystal

Mary Broad
By
Linda Crystal

Prologue
Believe It or Don't!

My intention in writing this book is not to convert you into believing reincarnation. Through my training in hypnosis we are taught that phenomenon exists, whether we like it or not, there are things that happen that are shrouded in mystery. We accept this and leave it alone, judgments in this area are not ours to make until more evidence or investigations are done in these areas. Phenomenon happens, all we can do is look at it closely when it happens and get the most out of it that we can. So I'm not asking you to believe my story, I don't care whether you do or not. This account happened to me and that's all there is to it.

I myself, have always been skeptical about reincarnation, but was fascinated by the scenario. So the question for everyone out there is: Did I, myself, live before? If I did in fact live before: What or who was I? I know that some time in your life you may have asked yourself these same questions and then went on with your life, wondering. That's usually the extent of one's exploration of reincarnation.

Mary Broad By Linda Crystal

Some of you may be interested in hypnosis and past life regression and have delved deeper in the subject, maybe even, having a regression yourself. For you folks this book will be fascinating and may inspire you to continue searching for your own past lives, if they exist. Skeptics be my guest and question everything I tell you in this book, because I'm open to discussions on this most profound experience.

In 1992 I decided that I wanted to become a hypnotherapist and sought out different schools to attend. I had no idea what was about to happen to me. I innocently took the classes and learned and studied as much as I could and absorbed in an effort to be a better than average hypnotherapist. Taking

classes in something you're really interested in, is

really exciting and all of this information was giving

me energy to see a goal of opening my own office

someday, I was esthetic, to say the least. What

happened next changed my life.

Mary Broad By Linda Crystal

Table of Contents

Mary Broad By Linda Crystal

Chapter 1

The Dream

Mary Broad By Linda Crystal

The dream came one night January 1993, when I least expected it. Dreams happen. They are not planned. Except that, when the dream was happening, I was fully aware that I was watching events unfold from inside a body, that wasn't mine. The dream unfolded like this.

I was getting off what I thought to be was, a school bus, (I can think in the dream and know the time frame is 1990's) although I didn't see one, I had the feeling of the presence of some sort of black vehicle, like a bus or vehicle, to my left side. I was a young girl, in my early teens, thin, I felt tall with thick, straight, dark hair, to around my ears, parted in the middle with bangs. I looked at my feet and saw a brown kind of loafer or slip on. I had socks on

and a dress that wasn't very colorful, black and

white print or check. There was something over my

shoulders like a wrap of some kind and I felt cold. It

was the fall and it was getting dark early. I looked

around and remember thinking, where am I? I could

see a muddy path winding off in front of me, with

some kind of trailers, people were packing, and I felt

that they were gypsies from the Pan American

Exposition. I was standing on a sort of hill looking

down. I could see the tops of the Pan American

Exposition, being torn down. The tops were green

and the workers were rushing around to get the

buildings down. They seemed in a hurry to get the

buildings down; they wanted them down, out of the

way, behind them. I knew the Pan American

Mary Broad By Linda Crystal

Exposition was being torn down early in the dream. I saw a coppery green dome, to be exact, that stood out in my mind. Something was sad and didn't feel right. Something had happened. The Pan American Exposition was a failure?

Meanwhile three or four girls came running up to me, calling, "Mary, Mary, come on, it's getting dark", and they came up close and one looked directly in my eyes and I could see she felt something was wrong with me. All I could do was stare back at them, speechless, wondering why were they calling me Mary, thinking, my name is Linda. It's like I was frozen and couldn't speak while I was trying to sort all of this out. Mary, I thought and in an instant I knew my last name started with a B, a short name. The girls were all around me now and one with long blonde curly locked hair grabbed my hand and pulled me forward. "Come on Mary; go home before it gets too dark".

I finally spoke and said;" I don't know where I live". The girl started to laugh and must have thought I was joking and replied," sure you do Mary, you live right over there on the corner", and she spun around and pointed to the left of my front. I could see the white peak of a house and lots of bushes and trees and it seemed to be very remote location. I then began getting flashes of the numbers 14 and 26.

Mary Broad By Linda Crystal

With my books in my arms, the tall way up, I also had a sense that I, as Mary, was poor. I was very scared now and saw a street sign to my left and I crossed the street, came right up to the street sign and had to look up to see the letters. It read Summer. I was on a hill, on a corner. It seemed to me that the Pan American Exposition had something to do with a zoo, and animals. I felt the general consensus of the people was that it was a shame to tear those beautiful buildings down for some reason.

My clothes seemed old and not very new and I felt poor and I knew I didn't live in the nicest house on the street. I was getting cold and it was getting darker and I started to walk in what I thought was my direction home. One girl then took me by the hand and said she would help me and kind of led me some of the way. I told her I didn't know the house and said she would go and find a policeman.

A man came walking up to me in regular clothes and at first tried to be kind. He had reddish blonde hair, seemed to be middle aged and had a short sleeved shirt on. He took me by the hand and said he would help me, but began walking in a completely different direction. It was really getting dark now and he told me he was a policeman. I asked him," If you're a policeman why don't you have a uniform on"? He only held my hand tighter.

Mary Broad By Linda Crystal

We kept walking and went down a winding stone staircase and when we got down to the bottom he sat down and opened his pants and pulled his penis out and made me perform oral sex on him. I was scared to death now and knew I had to follow his orders.

When he was done, he walked me to a small building that had a wooden door. He opened the door and pulled me in. It was all old stones, damp and one small window at the top, but it was a permanent window. When we got inside he left through another door at the opposite side, leaving me alone in the room. The doors were wooden and rounded at the top and there was one step up in front of each door. The room itself was recessed. I began climbing the wall in an attempt to reach the window,

but I was way too short to reach. I looked around,

the room was empty and I became frantic and started

crying. I remembered thinking in the dream that I'm

Linda, my name is Linda, and this is only a dream.

In the dream itself I couldn't wake up. I consciously

tried to get out of the dream and couldn't. I really

began to panic even though I knew I was in a dream,

and that I couldn't wake up. I knew Mary died in this

room. I also knew it took a week or more for her to

die. No one came. I, Mary, clawed at the window

with my fingernails.

When I woke up it was a surprise and a relief and

I immediately knew something profound, different,

special, unique, whatever you want to call it, had

happened to me. I got up and had some coffee and thought some more on the dream. I got on my computer and documented it right away because of the impact. When my husband got up, I told him. That was it; I couldn't stop thinking about the dream. I knew right away it wasn't just a dream. Not when you know you're in the dream, in someone else's body and then you can't get out. This was too much. It wasn't until months later that I made startling discoveries.

The dream would not leave me alone. I thought about it and could not figure out what I had experienced. Who was Mary? Why was I inside her body?

Chapter 2

Startling Discoveries

Mary Broad By Linda Crystal

Months went by and I continued my studies in hypnosis. I bounced the dream off a few of my friends to get their input and they were quite surprised when I unfolded the story. I told my relatives and couldn't stop thinking about me being inside the body of another person. It was quite different. I was actually looking out of someone else's eyeballs. This was enough to send shivers for sure down your spine. The dream became a constant until one of my hypnosis classes touched on something.

Spontaneous regressions. A regression that happens without provocation to an earlier time. ANY earlier time. It's like something opens a door and out this information pops. A sort of dejavue. I know I was working with relaxation and the conscious and subconscious minds a lot and maybe this strengthened my brain or unleashed a power or memory somehow. A past life? This is the closest explanation that I could come to and now it all seemed to fit.

The dream gave me a lot of exact information like the name of the street; was Summer, the girl's name; Mary B., and one day in August of 1993 I was in downtown Buffalo, paying my water bill. There on the counter by the window was a copy of a newspaper named "New York Antiques", I stared in shock at the cover, and it was a picture of the Pan American Exposition! I grabbed the paper and started looking for the article and the article gave the dates to 1901. I took the paper out to the car and couldn't believe my eyes. The buildings were just like the ones I saw in my dream. This gave me a very eerie feeling and now I knew I had to continue to search. Here I will confess, I hated history. It was my worst subject. It was so boring. I failed History.

Soon after that I went to my local library to look at old city directories. I had to ask the librarian to unlock the door so that I could go into the Special Collection Reference Room. All the books in there were old and out of print. I had been doing genealogy for the family so I knew the directories were here. It seemed damp and musty, old, very old.

Mary Broad By Linda Crystal

The Buffalo Name and Address Books from the late 1800's look like little diaries and they are that small. I looked up Summer Street and for the last name that started with a B, a short name. The directories then had the same idea about listing the family members, as they do today. There to my total shock and surprise was the name Miss Mary Broad, the second house on the corner of Elmwood and Summer, the number made me gasp, it was 260! The same number as my own house number! This was getting pretty scary now. I made copies of the pages to take home and couldn't stop staring at the papers. What was this whole thing about? I didn't have the answers, but I knew I wasn't finished yet. How could this all be happening?

While I was still in the library I found another set of little books called Dan's Blue Books of Society. These books had listed all the important people of wealth and status in the community. I remembered that I felt poor in the dream and thought okay, if I was poor then I wouldn't as Mary Broad be listed and guess what? The Broad family wasn't there. Coincidence?

I started telling my husband as I went along on my quest, what I had begun finding and showed him the pages from the address books. He was dumb founded. How could this be? Neither of us had answers or could believe what was unfolding.

Disbelief, I don't think so. The more I looked, the more I found.

The address book listed several other names that must have been siblings, Miss Margaret Broad, Miss Elizabeth Broad and at a later date Miss Agnes Broad. So these may have been my sisters. Now I wondered if those were the girls that came running up to me in the dream.

There was another book in the library about the Pan American Exposition by Austin Fox. It was called "Symbol and Show, The Pan American Exposition of 1901". Now I was thinking about how bad I was in history all these years and that maybe if

Mary Broad By Linda Crystal

I would have absorbed some of my classes, maybe
that would have helped me, but fail I did in history
and it became my all time stumbling block in high
school when they gave me two history periods in a
row; a classroom period and then a lecture period. I
failed miserably. It was so dull and boring and filled
with dates that I thought too trivial to be important.
Now I could kick myself. If any of my history
teachers are reading this book, they can vouch for
my lack of interest especially in history. The book
about the Pan American Exposition began to tell me
some more facts about the event that proved to be
chilling. According to the book the Exposition was
torn down early for a number of reasons. One was
the *assassination of President McKinley on

Mary Broad By Linda Crystal

September 6, 1901. **The other reason is that the weather was actually chilly and rainy.

The presence of gypsies at the Exposition was also a true fact. They were called the ***Zanzigs and were actually on the midway doing readings according to "Show and Symbol, the Pan-American Exposition of 1901".

My next step was to visit the Buffalo Historical Society to see what I could find. This trip became the complete turning point of the whole experience. It was here that I discovered a video, on the Pan-American Exposition, completely by mistake. I came for the library and asked for the person who was a specialist about the Exposition. I actually told

this woman about the dream. The woman replied

there is a video on file that was free to rent, about

the Pan American Exposition. I savored the video

and used the library section of the Historical

Society, but I already had a late start because the

hours in this library are very limited, so I didn't have

much time to investigate. The librarian gave me the

run down on where things were and I was promptly

issued a white pair of gloves to protect the items in

the library.

I looked over the city directories and found the

names of a few newspapers of the time and saw a

man looking at photos, so I got the idea that maybe

there were photos

on file. I asked the librarian about the photographs

and what kind the Historical Building carries and

she told me that basic real estate photos were kept or

left by families to preserve the architecture of the

various periods. She asked me the address of the

property I was asking about and I quickly told her

260 Summer St., Buffalo, with a lump in my throat

and then I held my breath.

Although the librarian came back with a negative

reply on 260 Summer, she did have the residence

next door and across the street from that same

address. I was thrilled and looked at the photographs

carefully to see if I could trigger any more memories

or thoughts about the time period. I was fascinated

the entire time. I looked at the picture right up to

closing time and the librarian had to throw me out, I was so mesmerized. I apologized for my over zealous nature and left. I would have liked to have toured through a special exhibition the Historical Building was holding on the Pan American Exposition, but the halls were all closed for the day.

I still had the video and went directly home to watch it. What I saw and heard was amazing. All buildings were required by the contracting specifications to have green on them in honor of the water that flowed over Niagara Falls. Niagara Falls at the time was the big drawing card for the Buffalo area and it was a way to tie in the Exposition. Green was the color I saw in the dream on the buildings, another confirmation. How could this be happening?

Mary Broad By Linda Crystal

This is all I could keep thinking. How would I know all this stuff from another era? An era I didn't live in. Or did I, as Mary Broad?

The location of the actual Pan American Exposition was another bombshell to me. At the time the Rumsey Farm, a 350-acre farm was leased for the Exposition. It actually embraced the lands approximately bounded by Nottingham, Elmwood, the Belt Line north of Hertel and Delaware. Delaware Park and the Zoo now occupy some of the land that the Exposition occupied. It was known as Nye Park in the 20's, named after the developer Sylvanus B. Nye. The map included in the picture section is directly from "Show and Symbol, The Pan American Exposition of 1901".

Mary Broad By Linda Crystal

The actual location of the Pan American Exposition had surprised me because I have had a thing about Delaware Park. I never liked to go there all these years, and as a citizen of Buffalo this was hard, due to the amount of events over the years that have been held there. I went walking once with a relative and the bridges through out the park always freaked me out. Scared me like something was about to happen, like a rape or something evil. When I went to the zoo the same thing happened. It was the stones of the displays for the animal shelters and the duck pond built of the stones and the various low protective walls that kept getting to me. There was something about those stones. I became so taken by these walls that I actually started drawing and painting them over the years, even before I knew what they had meant. It seems that a lot of the debris from The Pan American Exposition was used for Delaware Park and the Zoo. They both now occupy some of the land that the Exposition occupied. It was known as Nye Park in the 20's, named after the developer Sylvan us B. Nye.

When I found the name of Mary Broad and the address of 260, which was the same address of my own house number, chills ran through my entire body. How could this whole thing be happening? It didn't seem real. I came away from the library drained and confused, curious as to what else I might find. The dream persisted and kept rolling over and over in my mind. I couldn't get it out of my mind. Looking out from someone else's eyes is quite an experience and the show "Leap of Faith" came on toward the end of this discovery, which made me more aware of what was happening to me.

People around me began to notice that I had changed my attitude and that something was obviously bothering me that I was so deep in thought all the time. It's like a mystery is dropped on your doorstep and you have no choice but try to uncover an explanation. For a while it consumed all my energy. I knew there was more, lots more to uncover. I guess I had to follow the mystery. See how far it would all go. What else would I uncover?

Chapter 3

The House

Mary Broad By Linda Crystal

Thursday, Sept 16, 1993, it was a cool 40 degrees, overcast and rain was in the air. It was a very dreary day and fall was on the wing. It was very early in the morning and I had dropped my husband off at work so I could have the vehicle for the day. As I left him off at the warehouse I knew that today was the day that I would ride down Summer Street to see what I could see. There weren't any pictures in the Historical Museum Library files, so I expected to find an empty lot. I did this with the expectation that this was the end of the story, what I found took me by surprise.

As I watched the numbers get nearer to the address I was looking for, I slowed down to almost a crawl and traffic behind me began to sound their horns over my lingering. In the middle of the street I hit my brakes and stared at the number 260 and the house, it was exactly the same color I was now painting my house, a light yellow-beige with ivory trim. It was also a two family the same as mine, upper and lower, with an identical additional lot just like mine on Keystone Street. What the heck was going on? I am sorry but this was more than coincidences to a previous life.

Could ALL these things be coincidences? The driveway was to the left like mine, bushes lined the property like mine, the garage was a larger than usual one like mine and it looked like the rooms inside might also be set up like mine, but even at this point I have not been inside the house.

Mary Broad By Linda Crystal

I sat out in the truck and just stared at the house. I brought my camera and took pictures, so people could see I was not imagining all of this.

There were some houses in the area that had walls made of those stones again, they were everywhere in this area. I pulled in the parking lot across the street and

wanted to get a better look. All of a sudden I got this tremendous headache, my whole head felt like it was in a vice. Inside my head I heard a screen door slam, but no one came out of the house, but it seemed to come from the upstairs door. Now a smell came over the truck, a heavy paint smell, lacquer paint, it made me sick and I began to get nauseous. I felt sick from the paint smell, the same thing that has been

happening to me since I was a baby. No matter who

was painting when I was growing up, a house, room

or paint by numbers pictures I used to throw up

violently around paint. Today I have to use odorless

paint and thinner or else I become ill. I felt that it

was all connected to the house.

I knew the house was not owned by a wealthy

family because it was wooden, like mine on

Keystone Street. I also remember feeling poor in the

dream. As it turns out

just about every other house on Summer Street is

like a mansion, with pillars and built of brick and

stones. This particular house didn't seem to fit in

with the others on

the street.

When I was dropped off in the dream from

school, I was at an angle to the house and there was

a slight hill, the same landscape exists there now.

No wonder I was dropped off right at that corner, I

lived right there.

While I was still in my truck looking at the house

I could see all my sisters getting the dinning room

table ready for dinner. All the girls were in steps I

seemed to be the younger one. Maybe these girls

that came up to me in the dream were my sisters. I

have always wanted a big family with lots of kids, maybe this is why. When I stopped thinking about the house the headache vanished. Once I started to write again in the notebook, the headache returned. It took me awhile to regain my composure to drive and I felt as if I didn't want to leave, but that I wanted to go in the house. I felt like I was home. It was very clear to me with the information that I seemed to already know, that I had a connection to Mary Broad and that house.

I thought that the sight of the house would maybe put the dream to bed or that the empty lot would be the end of the road. I did not expect that the house was going to look exactly like my own. This was a shock that took my entire system quite awhile to absorb. Put yourself in my shoes at this time and quandary that I was in. Would you let the dream just go, as vivid and precise that it was? Did you ever have a dream you couldn't get yourself out of or couldn't end and wake up? How about being in someone else's body in a dream? The dream and circumstances were larger than life and I couldn't just pass them off. When I first went to the library and found Mary's name, I knew then that something was going on.

The house opened up a lot of questions for me, like who lived there now? Who were my parents? Another trip to the library was in order. I went right away; the suspense of this whole thing was unimaginable. I went immediately to the directories.

There I found that Mary's father's name was Thomas, my husband's name today. Thomas, Mary's father, was a painter of houses. Wouldn't the paint way back then been made of lacquer? Is the smell of lacquer paint connected to the house and Mary Broad, connected to my nausea?

I looked in the directories and found the name of the current owner and tried to call him several times but could never get through. I wrote him a letter but never mailed it, because for some reason I couldn't face at that time any more information about the dream. It actually took me several years to write this book and go back to call and interview some of the current living persons involved in the dream, Mary Broad's house, family and life.

It occurred to me at that time that President McKinley was assassinated at the Pan American Exposition while I was alive as Mary Broad and then President Kennedy was assassinated while I'm alive in this life. The house and thoughts of smells and sounds that happened to me while I was sitting in the truck played on my mind and other flashes now began to happen to me.

I drew these scenes whenever they occurred and are located in the picture section of this book. A picture of me, a woman that I believe was my mother, a little black change purse, a hat and the front of a porch. The year 1860 is very significant but I haven't gotten to find out what yet. Also the name Yankevich is connected to Mary Broad.

I'm still hoping now to interview the man that lives at the house and maybe get a glimpse of the inside to see if this unlocks any other memories. I did do some checking to find his name and that he is a musician. I do believe I left a message for him to call me, but he never responded. Maybe it freaked him out. I don't know. Funny I am a singer. The actual house is on the cover of this book.

Mary Broad By Linda Crystal

The mystery is still unfolding for me, but while I put the house on hold, I went on to another journey that is even still more astounding.

Chapter 4

Grave Hunting

Mary Broad By Linda Crystal

If Mary Broad truly existed and I knew she had, then she had to be buried somewhere. I knew that she had died young and that it would be around the turn of the century, late 1800s or early 1900s. I compiled a list of all the cemeteries that were in existence with the help of the directories and began a search. With each cemetery I gained some knowledge of the area, the peoples of that time and an idea of where Mary might be resting. This search went on for months, as I was doing this work as well as my schoolwork and working, taking care of my home and husband at the time, grandchildren and two sick parents. Each time I waited on the phone line with anticipation of finding Mary Broad's grave and then was discouraged when the search came back negative.

Mary Broad By Linda Crystal

I got so used to getting negative replies from cemeteries that I was expecting another no to come across the phone line. To my surprise this time was different. I'm the person that does genealogy for the family tree and I happened to be working on that project when I came across Holy Cross Cemetery in South Buffalo.

Almost a year after the dream on September 17, 1993, I made a phone call to Holy Cross Cemetery in South Buffalo. A lady named Alice answered the phone. I asked her about Mary Broad and told her that she died early around the late 1800s or early 1900s. Alice asked me if I was a relative and I answered no. Alice asked me how I knew she died as a child and I told her the story. There was silence at the other end of the line and then she replied, "She's here, you're right, she died at the age of 16," and she gave me the location of her grave. I then asked how long the cemetery was open that day. It closed early and I wasn't able to get there until the weekend.

My husband although mystified by all this reluctantly came with me to the cemetery that weekend. I remembered Alice had told me the area and that it was the oldest part of the cemetery. I forgot to ask about a headstone, but figured if I had been poor as Mary Broad there probably wasn't going to be a headstone.

Mary Broad By Linda Crystal

My husband and I kind of had the right location and then all of a sudden I felt like someone hit me in the chest with a shovel and I grabbed my chest, my husband came running over to me, worried and upset and I knew Mary Broad was right beneath my feet. We marked the spot to see if I was right. The area we were in didn't even look like people were buried there because there were hardly any headstones at all. It appeared more like just an ordinary hill in a park. I knew she was there. That day was a turning point for me, as it proved she existed and I was standing above her, all because of a dream.

Mary Broad By Linda Crystal

When I called Alice in the cemetery office the following Monday, she informed me that it would be a couple of weeks before she could get Ron, the specialist that worked in that old part of the cemetery to actually mark out and show me the grave. Those two weeks dragged by.

At the cemetery, the chill of fall was once again in the air and it always seemed like I was seeking her out in the fall. Here I will tell you that I never liked fall and always seemed to get very depressed at this time of the year. This has gone on my entire life. Sadness comes over me and until the spring, I fight with the blues. Is there a reason for this connected to Mary Broad? I already know it was fall that I was standing on the hill on Summer Street,

Buffalo and girls were calling me Mary. That

sadness was everywhere because the Pan American

Exposition was being ripped down and the President

had been shot and killed during this time. It was also

fall that President Kennedy was shot and killed in

Texas, November 22nd.

I feel Mary, the sadness of my passing, the

illness. Is it

another coincidence that every fall I become ill at

this time? Mary died in the fall, I discovered her

grave in the fall and fall always feels the same to

me. Not just an ordinary sadness sweeps over me.

It's more like a grieving period that I go through and

have since I was a child. Maybe Mary is the reason

why. The discovery of her grave is worth more than a diamond to me, all because of a dream. To me it's like a miracle, a magical journey that not many get to see.

I pulled into the cemetery alone, my husband was at work and I parked near the old part of the cemetery where I had assumed that I myself found Mary Broad's burial spot. and a cool breeze rushed by me and gave me the chills. This was eerie to say the least and I even locked the door it was so weird, until I saw Ron, the man who was going to pinpoint Mary's grave for me, pulling up with a station wagon. I knew it was Ron and I was so excited to find out where Mary Broad was buried.

We introduced each other and Ron went on to tell me that the graves were much smaller back at the turn of the century. People were smaller. Ron explained that Mary Broad did not have a marker. This fact didn't surprise me much because I had already known our family (already feeling like I was in fact Mary) at that time was considered poor and that markers were expensive. I didn't expect one when my husband and I had been looking for Mary's grave before.

Ron went on to tell me that he had worked at the cemetery for quite a few years and he was the only one there that knew anything about this section of the cemetery, which was the oldest section. He even pointed out a Columbus monument that depicted a direct descendant of Christopher Columbus was buried in the cemetery.

We started walking in the direction of the small hill in the cemetery and I was holding my breath about the location to see if my feelings were correct. Ron started at the back of the area and started walking, as if in yardstick measures and was actually counting rows and then walked to the right toward me and stopped. He bent down and saw a mark on the ground and said, "You already knew she was buried here, you marked her grave with an x. How did you know this?" It was then that I explained the dream, the previous trip with my husband and what had happened to me, as Mary.

I wasn't sure how he was going to take what I just told him. I think any person would look at me sideways with what I had just said but he replied," this is a cemetery; there are a lot of ghost stories from this place". It was at this point that I had asked him about tunnels being located under the Basilica and the hospital across the street. He was surprised by my question and said how do you know about those? I replied, another dream I had.

Mary Broad By Linda Crystal

The information that I received here at Mary's grave, the feelings and mental impressions, tell me that the mysterious journey isn't over. I now have Mary's exact date of death. November 22, 1878! Is it another coincidence that it happens to be a date that President Kennedy was assassinated on?

When I told Alice, the kind lady at the cemetery that Mary had died early, she thought I was a relative because I had details about Mary's death, that only a relative would have known. Alice didn't know that she could have been talking to Mary Broad herself. I often wonder if she thought about that sometime later, after she hung up from our conversation.

Alice also told me that it indeed took Mary awhile to die, 7 days to be exact, as she had Acute Meningitis. When I was born, I was a very sick infant, high fevers, chronic bronchitis, headaches and vomiting. Look at a medical book and these are some symptoms of meningitis. After the age of 16, I improved in health, to become pretty active and energetic, but was still plagued with extreme headaches, especially around paint and vomiting, but with bad chest colds. If you had been rushed to the

Doctor's office and hospital as much as I was, when I was little, you would have thought that I might not reach the age of 16.

The trip to the cemetery gave me so much information, I vowed to return and put a marker on her grave. I also felt compelled to keep going on with the search. I am using the word compelled because this was just not some normal want. You see a dress or article of clothing or even a car, you want it, but are using other reasons and Justifications for having it. This dream of Mary, her life, her death was a fascinating journey that many never get to experience. Prior to this I didn't even believe reincarnation was possible. Now I am convinced something else is at work.

Mary Broad By Linda Crystal

I did not have a choice in investigating this peculiar situation. I was compelled once I saw the library listing for Mary Broad. I only know that the more I investigated, the more I found out things that were pretty strange and comparable to my life, and quite possibly prove that we DO live various lives.

The fact remains, I had the dream and information revealed in the dream allowed me information that was uncanny. I found Mary's grave that in itself is amazing, she lived, but there's more. The exact location of Mary Broad's grave is Section 2, Row B, and Grave 24, Holy Cross Cemetery, Buffalo, New York.

Mary Broad By Linda Crystal

I knew my next trip was downtown Buffalo, to the Vital

Statistics Office for the Death Certificate.

Chapter 5

Death Certificate

Mary Broad By Linda Crystal

Any trip to downtown Buffalo is challenging, to say the least. The traffic is heavy, the nerves are short and Buffalo City Hall sits right on a traffic circle. This all requires you to park a distance away. All the while I was walking; I was anticipating what was going to be on the death certificate. Was I going to get one? Did they have records that far back? What would be the information on it? Questions, questions, questions, kept going through my head.

The ride in the elevator seemed to go on forever. Then the walk down the lonely corridor with old wooden doors and glass insets. The echoes of the voices and the footsteps gave this particular trip to Vital Statistics an eerie backdrop.

Mary Broad By Linda Crystal

At the desk the woman asked me if I was a relative when I gave her the date of death to be searched. Of course I said yes, just in case there was a reason why she was asking the question.

The wait, seemed forever. Then the woman appeared from the back room, saying that for some reason the information in this death wasn't in the normal spot. She told me she had to search a special rare area. It was as if she was warning me that maybe there wouldn't be a record. I have to tell you that the wait alone for this document was like waiting for the birth of a baby. It was like a time warp where time slowed down. The clerk then appeared and started apologizing.

The clerk started to explain that the document didn't exist but that she could give me a transcript. I accepted and handed the clerk the $10.00. The document was folded and put into a business envelope. Once again the trip back to the car seemed light years away. What was in the envelope?

When I opened the envelope, I found a statement that was hand written. The copy is at the end of this chapter. It stated that Mary A. Broad had died on November 22, 1878. Mary had died from Acute Meningitis that lasted for 7 days prior to her death. Mary was born in England, was 16 years old at death, one month and 12 days. This would place her birth around October 1862.

England, another questioned answered. Is this why I have been drawn to England, castles and royalty? At one point I could talk in a complete English accent during a regression that I had done by another hypnotherapist.

To top everything, I have married a man with the last name of

"Arthur", as in King Arthur. Their descendants are from Canada and obviously some were from England. I wondered if the stubborn trait was in the original

Arthur family? Mary Broad was from England!

Mary Broad By Linda Crystal

The address on the death certificate form also looked familiar because I remember I had knowledge of a number 14 and 26 in the dream. I took a ride down Adams Street, but the house at 141 Adams is no longer there. This is what I actually expected when I found Mary Broad's house at 260 Summer Street, Buffalo, NY. What happened to it? It seems that each piece of information I receive leaves another question for me. Why was I as Mary broad getting off the bus on Summer Street, if I lived at 141 Adams Street/

At this point in the search, I came to almost a complete stop. I know what I was reading on the certificate, but something wasn't adding up. The date of

Mary Broad By Linda Crystal

Mary's death was 1878. The Pan American Exposition was 1901. Through the eyes of Mary I knew a lot of information that came through AFTER Mary's death in 1901. How could that be? What was happening now?

Many people believe that in reincarnation, if you die early as a child, you return to the earthly world quickly (if you chose to do so). If you die as an elderly person, you may stay in spirit a very long time due to the fact that your mission here on earth has been completed. Studying spirit as long as I have, has given me a unique outlook on life. The spirit lives on and on until completion. The Spirit's Book has many answers that we cannot here on earth give without special guidance from the other side of life: people who have crossed over.

Did you ever notice that when a child dies in the family another is born to take it's place? Look at John Walsh for example and his son Adam. Shortly after Adam died another child was born. Making it possible that soul of the child could be in fact the one that passed away. I don't believe that one lifetime is enough to study this concept either, because you have to study one's complete life and we only physically live one life at a time.

Another situation in my in-laws family is the death of my mother-in-law's brother whose name was William. He was an alcoholic who died in a fiery car crash. Years later a boy was born to my mother-in-law and she named her son William. Doesn't he grow up to be in a horrible car accident, almost died and also has a problem with alcohol and also resembles the original William (her brother) that died in the car crash. Years earlier. Coincidence?

Another example, is the birth of the child shortly after the one Oklahoma bombing survivor lost her two sons in the blast. I could go on and on as I have many examples.

Was it possible than that I was TWO Mary Broads? The names in the little address book clearly state Mary Broad and that was 1900. There were clearly two Mary's born to the Broads, so what gives? Once again the questions kept popping up and the mystery kept getting more complex. So does life.

At least I found she lived, died, where she was buried and now that there might have actually been two Mary Broads born to the same family.

Mary Broad By Linda Crystal

CITY OF BUFFALO
NEW YORK

Division of Vital Statistics
David J. May
Deputy Registrar
613 City Hall
Buffalo, NY 14202
851-3844

TRANSCRIPT OF DEATH

NAME	Broad, Mary A
AGE	16 years 1 mo 12 days
SEX	Female
PLACE OF BIRTH	England
PARENTS/WHERE BORN	England
STREET	Adams
OCCUPATION	14
CAUSE OF DEATH	Acute Meningitis
DURATION OF SICKNESS	7 days
DATE OF DEATH	Nov. 27 1878
PHYSICIAN	F W Bartlett
SEXTON/UNDERTAKER	

Chapter 6
Drawings, Maps & Pictures

Mary Broad By Linda Crystal

Here is a link to the house today located at 260 Summer Street, Buffalo, NY.

http://maps.google.com/maps?q=260+Summer+St.,+Buffalo,NY&oe=utf-8&rls=org.mozilla:en-US:official&client=firefox-a&um=1&ie=UTF-8&hq=&hnear=0x89d312ff4a82ca5f:0xce783e358a558c63,260+Summer+St,+Buffalo,+NY+14201&gl=us&ei=nkzQTaSsKYLhOQHx09iHDg&sa=X&oi=geocode_result&ct=title&resnum=1&ved=0CCEQ8gEwAA

Here is where I (Mary Broad) was standing as the dream opened up and started to unfold. There is a bus top at the exact location, on the same side of the street today in 2011. Fact! Coincidence again?

http://maps.google.com/maps?q=260+Summer+St.,+Buffalo,NY&oe=utf-8&rls=org.mozilla:en-US:official&client=firefox-a&um=1&ie=UTF-8&hq=&hnear=0x89d312ff4a82ca5f:0xce783e358a558c63,260+Summer+St,+Buffalo,+NY+14201&gl=us&ei=nkzQTaSsKYLh0QHx09iHDg&sa=X&oi=geocode_result&ct=title&resnum=1&ved=0CCEQ8gEwAA

The view that I saw as Mary was a muddy road, rainy, dismal, sad, cold and getting dark picture of Summer Street in 1901.

Mary Broad By Linda Crystal

Here is a rough sketch I made of Mary Broad with the parted hair and bangs. I know I was very thin, lean and young. I though like 12, or 13 years old from what I looked like.

Mary Broad By Linda Crystal

Very Rough Sketch of Mary Broad

1993

Mary Broad By Linda Crystal

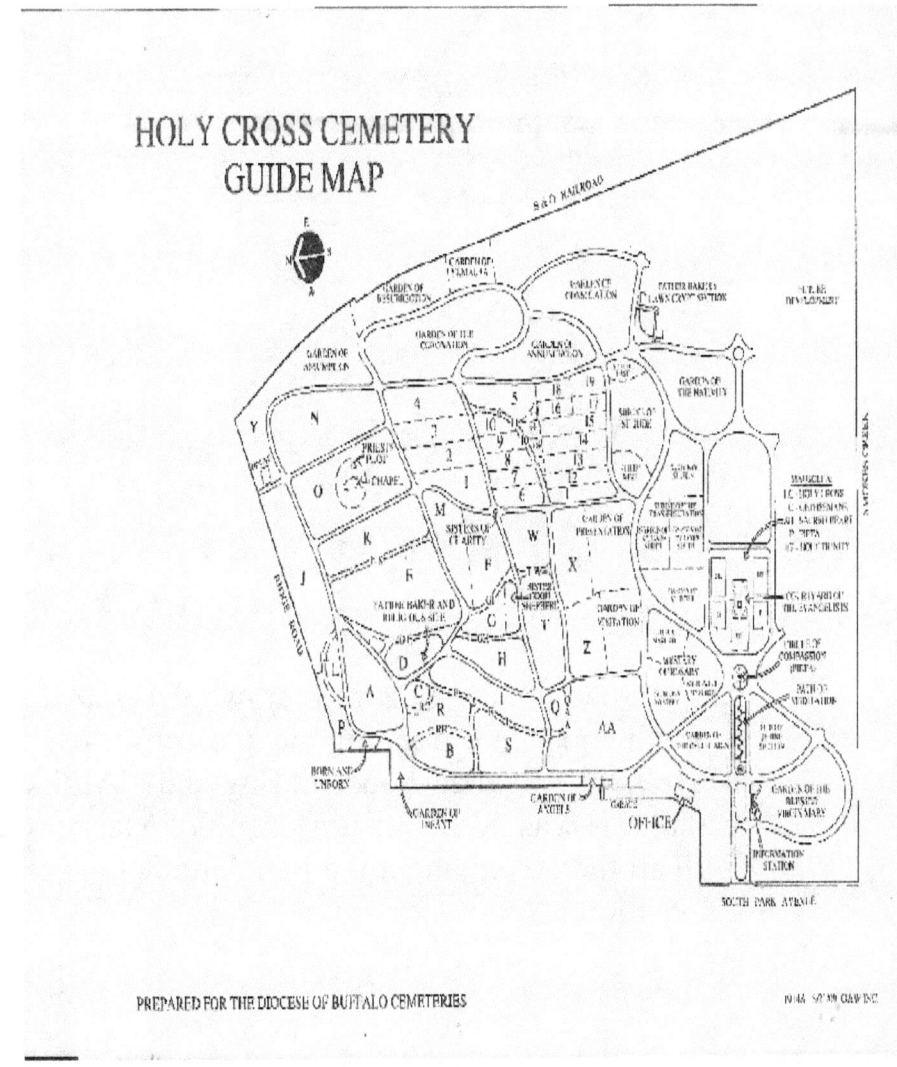

On the cemetery map, Mary Broad is in Section 2, Row B, and Grave 24

Mary Broad By Linda Crystal

Mary broad picture of a farm drawn 9/17/1993 as more dreams were flooding me and coming out. Maybe this was their house in England? All I know is that this was in the memory bank of Mary broad with all the others about the Pan American Exposition.

Memories flooded my brain from Mary, pouring out like an ocean. A lady with a tight perm or curly short hair, little tiny pearl earrings, laced collars, a small black scalloped change purse, the name Yankevich, the year 1860, brimmed hats with

Mary Broad By Linda Crystal

flowers, no make up. All of this information came through Mary Broad. There is information here today that I have not figured out.

Buffalo and Erie County Historical Society — Founded 1862
25 Nottingham Court · Buffalo, New York 14216 · ☎ 716-873-9644

EDUCATIONAL LOAN MATERIALS AGREEMENT

MATERIALS BORROWED: Pan-American Video "The Spirit Still Lives"

BORROWING DATE: 9 16 93   RETURN DATE: 9 23 93

BORROWER'S NAME: Linda Crystal

INSTITUTION: 260 Keystone St

ADDRESS: Buffalo NY 14211

TELEPHONE NUMBER: WORK ___ —   HOME 893 8013

LATE RETURNS WILL BE FINED $2 PER DAY.

As borrower of these materials, I will be responsible for their prompt pick up and return, and their security, plus I agree to the following:
If damage occurs, I will NOT attempt repairs.
I will not copy any slides or video tapes. (These materials are copyrighted.)
I will return the materials in the same condition that I received them. I will notify the museum of any changes or problems.

BORROWER'S SIGNATURE _____ date 9/16/93

(white copy-museum; yellow copy-borrower)

RETURNED ___/___/___   _____
          DATE   MUSEUM SIGNATURE

MATERIALS MAY BE BORROWED FOR UP TO 7 DAYS. SIGN OUT AND RETURN MATERIALS TO THE HISTORICAL SOCIETY OFFICE MONDAY THROUGH SATURDAY 10 AM TO 5 PM OR SUNDAY NOON TO 5 PM.

OFFICE USE ONLY:

CONDITION RETURNED _____

RETURNED ON TIME? YES   NO   AMOUNT OF FINE _____
                              DATE PAID ___/___/___

Mary Broad By Linda Crystal

The video rental agreement from the Erie County Historical Society clearly shows the date I rented this video to verify my dream information and also my address at the time of my dream began 260 Keystone St, one block over from a street called Sumner. Coincidence?

Mary Broad By Linda Crystal

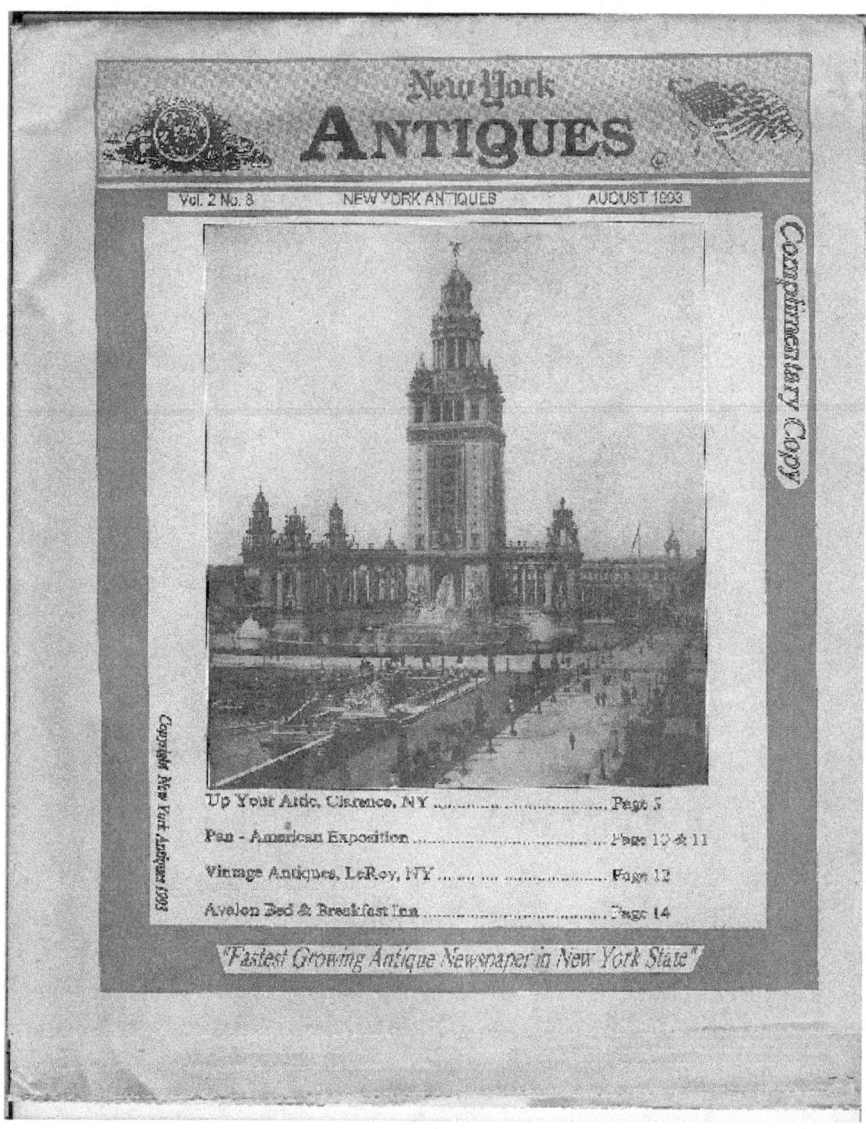

The copy of the newspaper that I saw about the Pan
American Exposition, which I knew nothing about
when the dream about Mary Broad occurred. Of
course after that I tried to verify the information in
my dream.

Mary Broad By Linda Crystal

32 Mr. and Mrs. William McNiven.
Miss Jeannette Owens Bryant.
34 Mr. and Mrs. Robert Barr.
Mr. William Barr.
Mr. and Mrs. Thomas K. Barr.
38 Mr. and Mrs. Jos. S. Van DeBon.
Miss Pearl Wood.
40 Mr. and Mrs. C. B. Armstrong.
Mr. and Mrs. A. B. Armstrong.
44 Mr. and Mrs. William H. Watts.
48 Dr. and Mrs. John Miller.
52 Mr. and Mrs. Timothy Gingras.
Mr. Albert T. Gingras.
Mrs. Cristine Tremill.

(Orton Pl.)

29 Miss Mary E. Johnson.
Miss Hattie P. F. Johnson.
33 Mr. and Mrs. E. O. Cheney.
Mr. Nelson Welch Cheney.
35 Mr. and Mrs. A. Judson Wells.
45 Mr. and Mrs. William C. Wells.
Miss Mercedes Wells.
Mr. Robert S. Sherman.
47 Mr. and Mrs. William S. Tweedy.
Mr. Osborne S. Tweedy.
51 Mr. and Mrs. John L. Cawson.
Mrs. H. A. Fray.

(Orton Pl.)

ST. PAUL STREET.

The streets in parentheses are cross streets.

(Main St.)

12 Mr. and Mrs. Rowland W. Hill.
Mrs. Fanny Dixon.
Mr. Henry S. Dixon.
14 Mrs. Mintie Lowery.
Mr. and Mrs. Harry Blakeley.
36 Mr. and Mrs. Albert P. Schen.

(Elliott St.)

(Main St.)

19 Mr. and Mrs. M. J. Smith.
23 Mr. and Mrs. Alfred R. Falck.

(Elliott St.)

SUMMER STREET.

The streets in parentheses are cross streets.

(Main St.)

8 Mr. and Mrs. Fred L. Beir.
Mr. Fred J. A. Beir.

(Linwood Ave.)

74 Mr. and Mrs. F. W. H. Forher.
78 Mr. and Mrs. T. M. Moore.
Mr. and Mrs. F. W. Sherman.

(Main St.)

19 Dr. and Mrs. H. J. Lino.
Mr. Lewis F. Lino.

(Linwood Ave.)

(Delaware Ave.)

137 Mr. & Mrs. Herman J. Roerner.

(Delaware Ave.)

148 Mr. and Mrs. William R. Brown.
Mr. William F. Brown.
Mr. George C. Brown.
Miss Nellie B. Brown.
158 Mr. and Mrs. Frederick Deming.
Mrs. Gertrude Biersenthal.
Miss Natalie Biersenthal.
164 Mr. and Mrs. G. H. Hughson.
172 Mr. and Mrs. Charles W. M. Iles.
Mr. and Mrs. H. T. Ramsdell.
178 Mr. and Mrs. J. B. Green.
190 Mr. and Mrs. P. H. Griffin.
Mr. Henry F. Griffin.
Mr. William A Griffin.
Miss Louise Griffin.
Mr. Edward B. McKenna.
200 Mr. and Mrs. Norris Morey.
Mr. Joseph H. Morey.
Mr. Arthur N. Morey.
Mr. Howard W. Morey.
Mr. and Mrs. Edward A. Barnes.
210 Mr. and Mrs. Edgar B. Jewett.
Miss Mabel Jewett.
216 Mr. and Mrs. E. L. Kimberly.
Mr. Ralph Kimberly.
Miss Louise Kimberly.
220 Mr. and Mrs. Charles F. Bishop.

(Elmwood Ave.)

254 Mr. and Mrs. J. C. R. Schultz.
Miss Eugenia A. Schultz.
Miss Bertha E. Schultz.
Miss Gertrude F. Schultz.
260 Mr. and Mrs. George Broad.
Miss Margaret Broad.
Miss Elizabeth Broad.
Miss Mary Broad.
Miss Agnes H. Broad.
262 Mr. and Mrs. Charles B. Huck.
Mr. Arthur C. G. Huck.
Mr. Theodore A. Huck.
Mr. Carl G. Huck.
264 Mr. and Mrs. H. R. Forbes.

165 Mr. and Mrs. Edward C. Hawks.
Mr. Maurice F. Hawks.
(Summer residence: Wingateshack, West Gloucester, Mass.)
173 Mr. and Mrs. Wm. H. Hotchkiss.
Miss Eleanor H. Hotchkiss.
Miss Margaret L. Hotchkiss.

(Oakland Pl.)

185 Mr. and Mrs. George C. Sweet.
Miss Gertrude C. Sweet.
Miss Laura Sweet.
Mr. and Mrs. N. L. Crittenden.
193 Mr. and Mrs. W. P. Osborne.
197 Mr. and Mrs. George L. Lewis.
Mrs. J. S. Sweet.
Mr. Everett L. Sweet.
211 Mr. and Mrs. Spencer Kellogg.
Miss Kellogg.
217 Mr. and Mrs. Henry R. Howland.
Miss Florence L. Howland.
221 Mrs. D. C. Weed.
Mr. George T. Weed.
Miss Weed.
Miss Edith Weed.
235 Mr. and Mrs. William J. Forsyth.

(Elmwood Ave.)

249 Mr. and Mrs. George R. Howard.
Miss S. H. Griffin.
Miss H. L. Griffin.
257 Mr. and Mrs. C. O. Howard.
Miss Lucia S. Howard.
263 Mr. and Mrs. Charles H. Utley.
Mrs. E. P. Each.
269 Mr. and Mrs. Henry J. Pierce.
Miss Violetta R. Pierce.

(Ashland Ave.)

283 Mr. and Mrs. Risley Tucker.
Miss Isabel McKibbin.
285 Mr. and Mrs. Walter F. Wilson.
Mr. W. Morse Wilson.
Miss Gertrude Wilson.
Miss Margaret Wilson.
295 Mr. and Mrs. Fred P. A. H. Stevens.

A combination of steel safes. MARINE BANK vaults.

MARINE BANK vaults preclude all danger from fire.

Mary Broad By Linda Crystal

The actual listing in the library stated 260 Summer
St
Miss Mary Broad
Mr. & Mrs. George Broad
Margaret Broad, Elizabeth Broad
Agnes Broad

I figured that Thomas Broad had to be a son

or relative to reside there at 260 Summer St, as he is

also listed at 141 Adams; however the house on

Adams is no longer there.

Chapter 7
A Live Connection

Mary Broad By Linda Crystal

There was a time that being a genealogist, I knew one of the best ways to find your relatives is to open the phone book and look at the names. That's exactly what I did. There in the current phone book for 1994 was the Broad Family. Alive and well, still living in Western New York after all these years. I called the one that looked like a name that was familiar to the line. They lived in East aurora, NY.

Mind you I had no idea what I was going to say or how to explain what has happened to me. A woman answered the phone. It was the middle of the day. She sounded older and I did not want to scare her. I introduced myself and told her that I had some information about relatives from a few generations ago. She said oh genealogy? And I said

Mary Broad By Linda Crystal

Kind of. I explained the dream Mary Broad and I said I am confused. I have one that lived during the Pan American Exposition and then I think there is another Mary Broad. The woman confirmed this for me. Two Mary Broads in the same family!!!! One died young and the family was so broken up over it, the named another girl after the first Mary. The second one became a teacher. I also explained there was a woman that wore her hair in tight curls and pearl earrings and she said yes you are talking about my mother and my family.

I explained the farm, the names and the illness and she said how did you get all this information on my family? That is when I tried to explain the dream to her. This seemed to shock her and she seemed to get upset. My intent was not to scare this poor woman, who may have really heard the story of a lifetime, but she was older and I have respect. I wanted to say I am Mary, your relative, but short of causing a real panic I said thank you for the confirmation and hung up. I am sure she could not grasp exactly what I was telling her. I heard Oh, Oh from her and I knew this was upsetting her. I said goodbye. You are never sure how someone would take this kind of information. She did confirm my suspicions that there were indeed two Mary Broads.

Was I both Mary Broads? The first one that didn't finish her life and then came back to live again? I had information from the death (1878) and the Pan American Exposition (1901). How do you explain that?

Than when I was younger growing up in Cheektowaga, NY I used to baby-sit for three small children. I had to walk down a street called Broad Street off Union Rd and every time I walked by the street sign I would stare at the name and say why does that name Broad seem so familiar to me. What is it about that name Broad? I was only 18 at that time when that was occurring. I did not have this dream for many years after that. But the street name bugged me.

The cover of the book is the actual house on Summer Street. I was never able to connect with the owner of the house and I may have left a message but never actually spoke with him about this situation. I tried to write letters but never mailed them. I was afraid that he would think that I was totally whacked about this dream happening. What's amazing is that the house still stands. The memories locked inside. I wanted to ask to see the inside but never got that far.

Chapter 8
More Dreams

Mary Broad By Linda Crystal

The original dream seemed to open the door for more information to come through. At first I was very upset that I could not get out of the first dream. It was real. It did not seem like a dream. It was frightening and I knew I died in that room and that it took me a long time to die and that I was young. I knew all this from the dream. I knew my name, but was Linda regressed I think. In a second I was awake. I had all this information prior to looking at the house, going to the library or doing any research at all.

I had forced myself to go to the library in the first place because the profound nature of the dream was too strong to let go. Then I thought it would satisfy me to see and find no resemblance to the dream. When I found the name Mary Broad at 260 Summer in the library address books I could not believe what I was seeing or experiencing.

At first I thought this had something to do with my grandmother, as her name was Mary. The more information was given to me and that I seemed to know automatically, it was clear this had nothing to do with my grandmother at all.

The dreams that followed were of a huge farm and house shaped like a barn. I dreamt of the pearl earrings, the change purse, and the year 1860. I still have not uncovered what was so important about that year. The brimmed hats and two different lace collars that were worn under blouses and shirts. The name Yankovich was also given to me and I have

not been able to place that name yet.

The call and trip to the cemetery said it all. I

told the woman I died young. I told her that it took

me a long time to die. I told her that there was no

head stone as my family was poor. What she did tell

me was that Mary was Scottish.

Chapter 9
The Search Goes On

Mary Broad By Linda Crystal

Although I have done oodles of searching for ancestors in my family tree, I had not yet had the experience of crossing the ocean to receive information on relatives. I wanted to see if I could find the birth certificate for Mary.

I have been to cemeteries hundreds of times tracking down information from head stones on my relatives. In this case Mary didn't have a headstone. There was no information there for me to gather and analyze. The Death Certificate was pretty outstanding to me as it was. However as I was driving through Forest Lawn Cemetery looking for one of my own relatives in real life I passed a marker that said BROAD. Here we go again. How could this be so close to the road and on my route that day? You can't tell me something isn't going

on here with Mary Broad.

I get out of the car and grab my camera and as

I walk over to the stone I see the names Thomas &

Ellen Broad, Section 14 (one of the numbers that

came to me on Summer St). This stone is huge. The

family could not afford a stone for Mary, but their

stone is beautiful. This had to be purchased by other

people for them. The years were 1842-1894, 1843-

1910. These folks were Mary's parents! I wasn't

even searching for them and this cemetery is

humungous to say the least. I am sorry but this is

hard for me to believe and I lived it.

Mary Broad By Linda Crystal

Chapter 10
Birth Certificate

Mary Broad By Linda Crystal

In 1998 some four (4) years later, my research on Mary Broad was still not over. The Internet was beginning to team with information on searching for your ancestors. This helped me immensely. I know Mary Broad came from England. I found an address to write to. The address is General Register Office, St. Catharine's House, 10 Kingsway, London, England WC2B6JP. I am putting this address here so that if anyone wants to look for a birth certificate for England, you will have the address.

To my surprise British Ancestors contacted me via email immediately. They had found a birth certificate for Mary Ann Broad! This news was over whelming for me at the time. I was so happy, relieved, and curious all at the same time.

Mary Broad By Linda Crystal

The registration District for the birth was Preston, Sub-District of Preston, County of Lancashire. Mary Ann Broad was born October 4, 1862. I had tried to figure backward from the death certificate and got to October 11th. I was close. Mary was born at 46 Brougham St. Name of the father was Thomas Broad. Name of the mother was Ellen Broad. Yet I found the marker first in my travels through Forest Lawn and knew what I had found before I received this information. Ellen's maiden name was Gordon. The date was now 2000. The cost was $50.00 to obtain this certificate.

Mary Broad By Linda Crystal

CL 885361

CERTIFIED COPY of an   ENTRY OF BIRTH
Pursuant to the Births and   Deaths Registration Act 1953

Registration District **PRESTON**

1862   Birth in the Sub-district of   Preston   In the **County of Lancaster**

Columns	When and where born	Name, if any	Sex	Name and surname of Father	Name, surname and maiden surname of mother	Occupation of Father	Signature, description and residence of informant	When registered	Signature of registrar	Name entered after registration
418	Fourth October 1862 46 Brougham Street	Mary Ann	Girl	Thomas Broad	Ellen Broad formerly Gordon	Tanner Journeyman	Thomas Broad Father 46 Brougham Street Preston	Eleventh October 1862	Henry Bradley Registrar	—

Certified to be a true copy of an entry in a register in my custody.

B. Nuttall   acp Superintendent Registrar

28th December 2000 Date

Here is a map to show you where Preston

is.

St. Peters Church, Preston, England was erected

in 1825 and was present when Mary Ann Broad

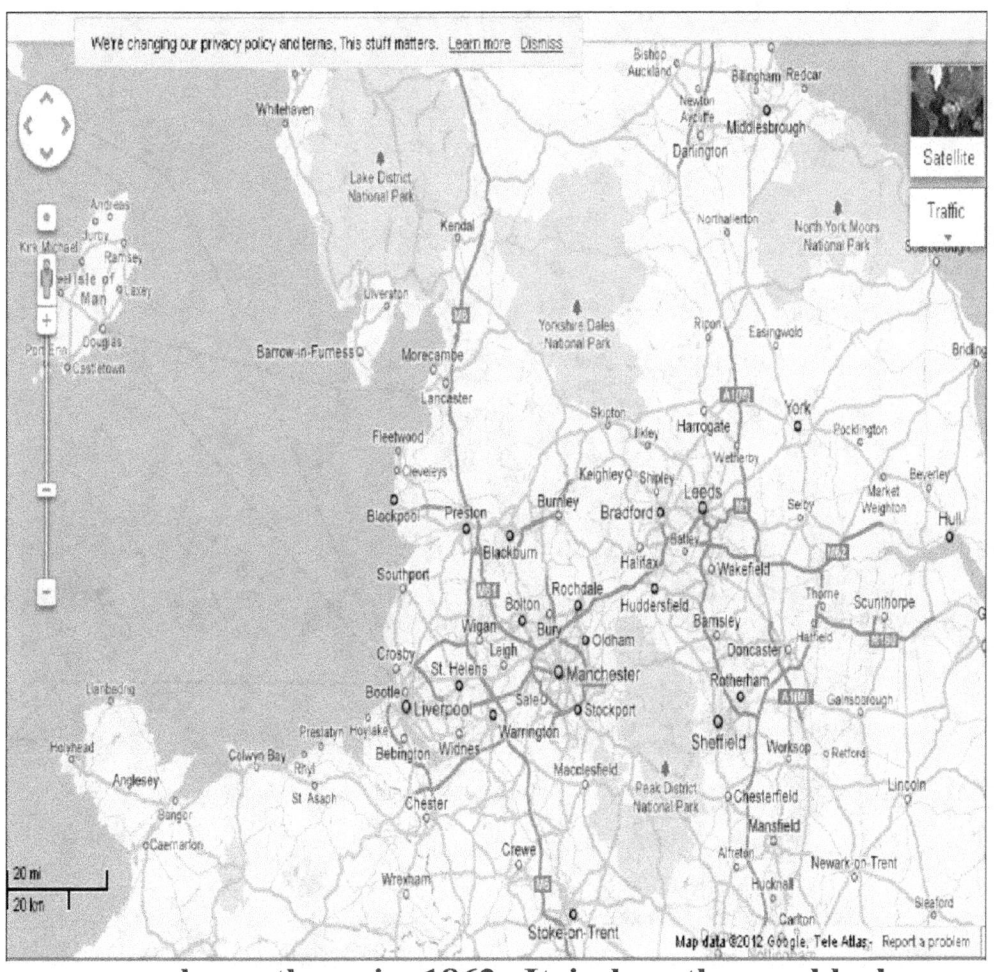

was born there in 1862. It is less than a block

from the University that took over Brougham St, which is no longer there. In 1831 there were 33,000 people in Preston. The church closed in 1973. The picture is from a Google search.

Mary Broad By Linda Crystal

Mary Broad had a short-lived life that took her from England to Buffalo, New York, where she will spend an eternity at Holy Cross Cemetery in Lackawanna, New York.

I did find out that Mary was Scottish and that is where the Scottish buried their dead during this period of time in Buffalo. I was told that she would have attended Holy Angels Church & Academy, which is now D'Youville College.

I would have never been aware of Mary Ann Broad if I hadn't had the dream that I did. It put me on a fascinating journey. This was a dream and an

experience that one cannot forget.

Chapter 11
More Confirmations

Mary Broad By Linda Crystal

      As I continued my research into Mary Ann Broad, I found more amazing things of interest. I have come to realize that some names are more powerful, or been used by living people over the years. Mary Ann Broad, Mary Broad is one of those names. It is extremely common. For example I just did a search on Ancestry and I am amazed at the amount of Mary Broads there were. It is a name that has been used and used over and over again. Many girls, women have been named Mary Broad. I myself seemed to see two lifetimes of a Mary Broad from the same family. This confirms a theory that I also read in The Spirits Book, that if a young person, child dies in the family; they recycle back to the same family to finish their life goal. Old people stay in spirit for a long time as they life mission may have been completed and are given a choice as to whether they want to return. I feel one lifetime is not enough to study this as a child is in a different container of a person to recognize the soul.

This I seemed to have experienced and have been watching myself. My grand father died a month before I was born. My cousin was born years later on the date my grandfather was born. This cousin, looks, feels and acts like my grandfather. Is he my grandfather's spirit?

My mother-in-law had a brother who died in a car accident. I did not know this until we were going over the family Bible and a newspaper article fell out. It showed the mangled mess of a car. My mother in law's brother was killed. He was drunk while driving. His name was William. My brother in law was born many years later and was named after the deceased Uncle "William". He too began to drink heavily and was hit by a semi tractor-trailer, but survived. Reincarnate? The accidents are almost similar. Progression is that this time he lived to finish a mission.

These are just a few examples. I actually have many as I have been doing research in this area for quite a long time.

Another confirmation for me is the hairstyle that I saw myself in with the bangs. I have found several newspaper clippings and the bangs fit right

in with the part down the middle of the head as well.

As I knew in the dream the Pan American

Exposition was closed down early for several

reason; the rain, the assassination and chilly

temperatures. This all confirmed in the video and

Pan American Exposition Book.

The brimmed hat I saw in the follow up

dream, the pearl earrings and the scalloped purse fit

the times. How would I know all this information?

The only thing that I have not been able to

find and confirm is the name Yankevich.

Chapter 12
Headstone For Mary

Mary Broad By Linda Crystal

This experience is a very profound experience for a person to have. I choose to write about it and let the readers see what happens. After all the research and investigation and time that has passed, I have promised Mary one thing. That if I wrote a book about her and my dream that I would buy her a headstone. Place it in the cemetery so that she is not forgotten. That she would be one Mary Broad that would shine. Maybe she lived a short life, but it was a powerful life. Maybe she was one of the many, I don't know. Through her, I saw two lifetimes.

I knew that when she died, the family did not have the money to properly mark her grave. I will now try to do that for her. Forever we are linked. It is very hard for me to grasp the similarities in our lives, houses and I do not believe they are just coincidences.

I went to visit her grave the other day and there was a heard of deer roaming through the cemetery. The Native Americans believe deer symbolize kindness and gentleness. They did not run. They all just stood and looked at me. I felt blessed to have seen such a sight.

Mary Ann Broad, Rest In Peace

Mary Broad By Linda Crystal

References

*'Show and Symbol, Pan American Exposition, pg. 28
**Show and Symbol, The Pan American Exposition, Of 1901", preface, pg. v
***"Show and Symbol, The Pan-American Exposition Of 1901", pg.98

Bibliography

Fox, Austin M., "Show and Symbol, The Pan American Exposition of 1901", Meyer Enterprises, 1987

"New York Antiques Newspaper",Volume 2, No. 8., August 1993., page 10 and 11.

"Spirit Still Lives", Pan American Video, property of Buffalo and Erie County Historical Society, Buffalo, N.Y., Rented 9/16/1993

"Dan's Blue Book of Society",

"Buffalo Name and Address Books"

Mary Broad By Linda Crystal

The Spirits Book

Catholic Cemeteries.com (Map of Holy Cross)

Antique Magazine

TV Programs

Leap Of Faith
Sunday Morning, CBS, Reincarnation, broadcast
5/15/2011

Internet Resources: Google Maps

Linda Crystal Bio

Blog Talk Radio Show Host
http://www.blogtalkradio.com/lindacrystal

www.lindacrystal.com

Mary Broad By Linda Crystal

BA Degree-State University of New York At Buffalo, Forensic Psychology, 1997

Certified Clinical Hypnotherapist: Atwood Institute for Research & Development, 1993

College of Divine Metaphysics; Fellowship, 1994

Forensic Astrologist

Author: Star Signs: Published Senior Beacon

"Who Killed Mandy?" Lulu.com

Passed NYS Exam Private Investigator:

ICS School of Law Enforcement

TV & Radio Personality: Daybreak at WHLD, WKBW, WECK, WJYE, WJJL Blog Talk Radio

Member Psychic Crime Fighters

Founder WNY Psychic Meetup Group 2007

Trained In Polygraph

Deception Training

Mary Broad By Linda Crystal

Graphologist

Psychic Fair Promoter

Mary Broad By Linda Crystal

Mary Broad By Linda Crystal